T0197473

TRIUMPHANT JOURNEY ROAD

Tragedy to Triumphant

D O R I S O. C O L E

AuthorHouse™
1663 Liberty Drive
Bloomington, IN 47403
www.authorhouse.com
Phone: 1 (833) 262-8899

Because of the dynamic nature of the Internet, any web addresses or links contained in this book may have changed since publication and may no longer be valid. The views expressed in this work are solely those of the author and do not necessarily reflect the views of the publisher, and the publisher hereby disclaims any responsibility for them.

This book is printed on acid-free paper.

ISBN: 978-1-7283-7190-0 (sc)
ISBN: 978-1-7283-7189-4 (e)

Library of Congress Control Number: 2020916377

Print information available on the last page.

Published by AuthorHouse 09/09/2020

authorHOUSE®

DEDICATION

To my children Kenny and Kerri, my grandchildren Luther and Aria and those on the way, Mr. & Mrs. Luther R. Cole Sr. (parents/deceased), Mr. & Mrs. Delma R. West (Mom, TJ, and Dad Del) my spiritual parents.

ACKNOWLEDGMENTS

Allison Williams aka Princess (sister/friend), Linda Osborne (friend/author), Phyllis Harris (friend/singer) and everyone who prayed, supported, and encouraged me.

FOREWORD

There are few people that we encounter on this amazing road called life, wherein once those paths are crossed you're better able to make sense of your departure because the person who crossed your path; became instrumental in helping you to not only understand your destiny but guided you in the way of your destination!

For me, Doris Cole became that person, thus making it much easier for me to understand the transition that God was ordering for my life. As you read *"Journey Travelers,"* board this book as you would as a passenger on a train, and allow the conductor to move and maneuver you through the mountainous terrains of life as she speaks from a place of various ports; to remind you that every view along the way should be valued because if you wait to exhale when you arrive at your destination-you'll miss the victories that God was giving you along the way. This jewel of a book reminded me, that you can make every journey regardless of the bumps, distance, potholes in the road; as long as you have some spiritual shocks to absorb the blows.!

- Eric D. White Sr. (Servant Leader)
"The House of Intercession"
Austin, Tx

CONGRATULATIONS!!! This is truly a special time in her life today that the Lord has made. Therefore, she can give thanks, rejoice and be glad in it. For God's Word (Ecclesiastes 7:8) says, "Better is the end of a thing than its beginning; the Patient in Spirit are better than the Proud in Spirit." Since this is her 1st Book Publication, I consider it a major accomplishment. To all those who are blessed to read this book I believe they will be totally astounded as to how all the Dots begin to connect, from the movie "The Wizard of Oz" with "Dorothy" the lead character, how her Dots connect to the Author of this book "Doris". It's a talented and gifted reading. I know Doris will continue on the narrow path with a sincere and powerful heart, full of Faith, Hope, Love and Joy while giving much Glory and Thanks to the Holy Spirit as she continues to pursue the final destination as she moves down The Triumphant Journey Road.

Your Dearest friend and Mom # 2,
T. J. West

TABLE OF CONTENTS

Foreword

Dedications and Acknowledgements

Introduction

1. **Triumphant Journey Story:**

Where Your Life's Journey Begins

2. **Disasters:**

STORMS - Sudden Turbulent Opposition Rattling our Mind and Soul

3. **DEEP Oasis:**

A Place of Refreshing, Relaxing, Rejuvenating, and Renewal -

Dorothy's "Somewhere Over the Rainbow" Experience

4. **Journey Road:**

The Yellow Brick Road – "Order My Steps"

5. **Journey Travelers:**

Who We Encounter Along the Way – Reason, Season or Lifetime?

6. **Renovations & Reinventing:**

Time of Transformation – "When God does a 'New Thing'"

7. **Triumphant:**

No Matter Where You Are in Life–
"Shout unto God with A Voice of Triumph"

SONG-LIST

"God's On Your Side" by Mississippi Mass Choir

"Holding On" (BETTER) by Hezekiah Walker Azusa – The Next Generation 2

"I Told the Storm" by Greg O'Quinn and Joyful Noyze

"My Soul Is Anchored" by Douglas Miller

"My Testimony" by Marvin Sapp

"Paradise" by Norman Brown

"Good Morning" by Mandisa

"Take Me To The King" by Tamela Mann

"I Don't Mind Waiting" – (*Passion*) by Juanita Bynum

"Hero" by Mariah Carey

"He's Preparing Me" (Extended Version) by Daryl Coley

"He Knows My Name" by Tasha Cobbs Leonard

"Deliver Me" (This Is My Exodus) by Donald Lawrence & Le'andria Johnson

"I Can Believe Again" by Larnell Harris

"Dream Again" by James Fortune

"We Fall Down" by Donnie McClurkin

"Great Is Your Mercy (LIVE)" by Donnie McClurkin

"Overflow" by Pastor William Murphy III

"Made A Way" by Travis Greene

"Triumphant" by Vashawn Mitchell

INTRODUCTION

My story and message come from an old-time classic, *The Wizard of Oz*, as God revealed to me how it relates today – the theme of old school to the new school. This classic has brought on a new revelation as well as an illustration of how our life is a journey, but it is more than just a journey, it is a triumphant journey. If it weren't for the storm that Dorothy encountered, she would have never known or realized that her life was, is, and will be triumphant.

I had not seen the movie in a while and was going to buy it or get it on *YouTube* for about $3.99, but I never got to it. This one day, I went to the library to do some school coursework, but before actually entering into the library, there was a room where they were selling books, tapes, and videos, so I decided to stop in and check it out. As I was glancing around from shelf to shelf, there was one shelf labeled videos that had DVDs, and right there in front of me was *The Wizard of Oz* on DVD, and it was only .50 cents.

I wanted to holler, "Look at God" like that song by Koryn Hawthone, "Won't He Do It." He says in Matthew 7:7,

"Ask and it will be given to you; seek and you will find; knock and the door will be opened to you (NIV). Another version puts it like this, *and so I tell you, keep on asking, and you will receive what you ask for. Keep on seeking, and you will find. Keep on knocking, and the door will be opened to you.* (NLT)

Do you remember *The Wizard of Oz*? If you can recall, when the movie starts, it starts with the MGM Lion roaring. Do you remember this Lion, the MGM productions, and music playing in? The background? Well, the Lion is still roaring as I am playing some Norman Brown Jazz in the background.

The story goes something like this. A tornado rips through Kansas, Dorothy (Judy Garland) and her dog Toto are whisked away in their house to the magical land of Oz, and they follow the Yellow Brick Road toward Emerald City to meet the Wizard. I am going to put it like this. Dorothy had to see the Wizard to obtain directions to get back home. We go to God for direction to find our way; so, the song, "Take Me to The King" by Tamela Mann, speaks of the King of Kings, where we can go our Way maker. Dorothy and Toto run down an isolated and desolate country road as they were being chased by a mean old lady, Miss Gulch, who is being depicted as the Wicked Witch of the West. At the beginning of the movie, before the storm and Dorothy transported to Oz, Auntie Em exchanged words with Miss Gulch, and you could tell that she wanted to go off or get something off her chest. She had been holding back. Ms. Gulch (the mean old lady) wanted to take Toto away from Dorothy so Auntie Em said to her, "For twenty-three years I have been dying to tell you what I thought of you, but being a Christian woman, I can't say it," and she walked away (watch the body language).

As I watched, I said to myself, "Get her Auntie Em." Now, if that were to happen in today's world and it was a Sista, she would have been snapping and popping that neck, and that hand would have been saying,

"I would give you a piece of my mind, so don't take me there!" It might have turned into an episode of the *Jerry Springer Show*. Well, you know the rest.

Dorothy appears to be raised by her aunt and uncle. It came to me that Dorothy did not have girlfriends, no one she could call and hang out with, call, and not sure if they even had a phone. Did you ever realize that even though she lived out in the middle of nowhere in a farmhouse with no neighbors in sight, Dorothy's hair always looked like she walked out of the salon? She was always groomed from head to toe with a touch of makeup. This made me think about myself and my tendency at times to look the way I feel. It reminds me that I need to keep it fresh as well – as they say, "Always be ready in season and out of season." She experienced a disaster, but it did not affect how she presented herself to the world.

She gets to her house and begins complaining and murmuring first to Auntie Em and Uncle Henry, and they give Dorothy that look your parents might have given you back in the day or may still give you today. You know that look, the gaze where they did not have to raise a hand, nor their voice. It is the look that says, "You need to find something to do, or you need to go somewhere." Next, she begins to complain and murmur to her other family members, and they began giving her advice, but she does not see it that way. Oftentimes, we do the same thing. Sometimes we are given advice, but it just goes in one ear and out of the other.

Meanwhile, no one is really paying her any attention, and therefore, she wants to run away to a place somewhere over the rainbow. The twister comes and sweeps everyone away and Dorothy can't forget about Toto (he is like her best friend), to that place somewhere over the rainbow. Dorothy doesn't realize that this is the beginning of her journey to the unknown, and everyone and everything she was about to encounter was according to God's purpose and plan. She didn't realize she would be transformed and reinvented along the way as she meets new people, visits new places, and experiences new things. On this journey, she gets a new perspective on life.

Well, before I take you along Dorothy's journey, let me tell you a little about me. I was born in Brooklyn, NY, and raised in Binghamton, New York, a city in upstate NY, to my parents, Mr. and Mrs. Luther R. Cole Sr., who are now deceased. Yes, I am a baby boomer in my 60s, but do not get it twisted, I am SAVED, SMART, SASSY, SOPHISTICATED, and still SEXY (holla at your girl). When I was growing up, marijuana – doobie, joint, spliff, or whatever you want to call it – was a big thing, and yes, I smoked it, but that was not my choice of drug. My drug of choice was cocaine (coke) and no, not the Coke that you drink. I snorted what they called white powder. Yes, thank God I was delivered, set free and now I drink wine and some cocktails now and then - do not judge me.

I love and enjoy listening to music on my Android. No, I am not an iPhone girl yet, maybe later.

When I'm tuned into Pandora, I listen to *I'm Every Woman, Norman Brown Radio, Smooth Jazz Radio,* and certainly my all-time favorite, Gospel – *Hezekiah Walker & The Love Fellowship.* I grew up on old school gospel music such as *What A Friend, I Need Thee, Precious Lord,* and *Sweet Hour of Prayer,* just to name a few. Donnie McClurkin has a nice old school medley, and oh, I cannot forget *Something About the Name Jesus* by The Rance Allen Group.

When it comes to dancing, I can break it down. Unfortunately, as I have gotten older, I cannot break it down as much, but I still try. That is how I met my ex-husband. He cleaned the church, and he loved music.

I worked in the office doing clerical work and would hear him playing music as he cleaned. When I heard him play music, I had a good time listening and dancing – moving to the beat (nothing unholy). When you read this book, you will see many references to songs, some with lyrics, and it will be a variety of music, as I said before love listening to music.

Writing has become my therapy, and God, my Therapist. I love to journal, and I write with no form or fashion. Sometimes my writings came from messages that I've heard, a thought that came to mind, something I've read, a movie I've seen, or things I'm going through, but there were times when they were God inspired by the Holy Spirit. I also like action movies like; *CREED* starring Michael Jordan and Sylvester Stallone, *Equalizer* with Denzel Washington, and *Sniper*: *Special Ops* with Steven Seagal – keep the action going!

Well, let us talk about my family. My dad worked as a metal polisher for a company called Kason Hardware, where he retired after forty years. My dad had hands like iron -- strong and heavy.

Trust and believe I had experienced them first-hand when I used to get spanked. There is a saying, "There is always one in every family," and I was that one. If you asked my brother and sister today, who both reside in North Carolina, they would agree. They would say, "Yep, she was the one - better her than us!"

My dad was also an impeccable dresser. His shirts and pants were ironed and not by the cleaners, he ironed and pressed his clothes with starch. His shoes shined, and he always had a manicured look despite his occupation. In his seventies, he served as a Deacon and Treasurer at Beautiful Plain Baptist Church. I remember his favorite song was *Victory is Mine*, and when he would hear that song, he would bounce and clap along having a good time in the Lord. Even when my dad was eighty-nine, he looked like he was in his early seventies. I have to say he was a handsome man, bull legged and smooth on his feet. He loved to dance plus back in the late fifties, he sang in a quartet in several upscale clubs in New York City. I believe that is where I got my love of dancing.

My mother would tell us how she met Dad, and it was so romantic. My parents met in the fifties, and my dad sang in a quartet in a fancy restaurant. My mother would order her food, and my dad would have the waiter cut her ham steak in bite-sized pieces. What you say?

Mom loved to shop and dress fashionably. Her thing was wigs – long, short, and some sassy. She worked for an elementary school for years and worked part-time, providing environmental services on a nearby college campus. In addition, she sang in the choir, her voice taking on new heights, depending on the song she was singing. Her favorite song was *It Is Well with My Soul*, and when she hit those high soprano notes, you could both hear and feel the anointing. Dad would love to hear her sing he would sit so proud, I could hear him say "yes, that is my wife." She would give us the best and taught us how to represent ourselves.

Both my parents were neat freaks. If you came over to visit, the house was always kept clean, as we all had chores, and there were no options, no negotiating, and you better not pout. It reminds me when the Bible says, "Do it as unto the Lord."

Well, you know every family has some dysfunction, whether they admit it or not. Every house, every home has a story, and what you see is not what it is. One more thing about family; we all have family members who we are close to, those we are distant from, those we try to ignore, those we don't really care about knowing, and some we don't know even exist. The bottom line is it still spells FAMILY. When it comes to family gatherings and events, everybody is everybody, and everything is everything. You will find some at the table playing Bid Whist, Dominoes, or Spades. You might even see some in a corner shooting dice. You cannot forget those that have the large or small red cup, the children running around, music playing, or the young and old sharing memories while laughing out loud. Then there goes the Electric slide and Soul Train line and nothing of significance matters anymore, just laughing, loving, and celebrating life – the bottom line, it spelled FAMILY. Remember that song "We Are Family?"

I will share more about me as we travel along this journey. While on the course of her journey, Dorothy meets the following as she is on her way to the Emerald City to see the Wizard.

- Scarecrow: Desires a brain – Do you know of anyone that needs to use their brains? They just do not think about things; they just react. Is this you in some area?

- Tinman: Desires a heart – Do you know of someone who has a hardened heart? Is this you in some area?

- Lion: Desires courage – Do you know of someone who is afraid of moving outside the box? They allow fear to keep them from moving forward. Is this you in some area?

Well, Dorothy (insert your name here) is on a journey, on this journey Dorothy (insert your name) has been instructed to follow the yellow brick road. Below are questions for you to consider as you go through your life journey:

1. Where is your journey taking you?
2. Who are you taking along with you on your journey?
3. What is your purpose for the journey?
4. When will you know you are there?
5. Why is it important?
6. How are you going to get there?

So, let us start our journey.

TRIUMPHANT JOURNEY STORY

You might be asking how I came up with this name. Let me tell you, it is not just a place, or a person, but the journey along the way to your destination. My journey began in Apalachin, NY, on an unpaved country like road in a house at the top of a hill. It was the home of my spiritual parents, Mrs. T.J. West, and Mr. Delma West. She is a retired Howard University Administrator, and he is a retired Lockheed Martin Engineer and Pastor of a nearby church. My natural parents were deceased when I was in my middle to my late forties. I was a member of my hometown church serving as an usher and sang in the choir when I met them. They were visiting guests as Pastor West was the preacher for morning service.

When TJ walked through the door to the church service, there was something about her. She had a stature about her; she was tall, beautiful, and was in a class of her own, she was queenly and confident as she walked down the aisle. She was articulate in speech, but most of all, she was a woman of God with a discerning spirit.

After we met and were introduced, weeks later, she had a woman's retreat at her home, and I was invited. As I accompanied another lady in her car, I thought as we were riding, "Where are we going?" We arrived at a house at the top of a hill, and it was a big house. I loved her kitchen, which was something I imagined having one day. There were around thirteen rooms or more (prayer, weight, family, etc.) The downstairs was like an apartment all by itself, and out back, there was a small pond, a lot of land, and trees. The retreat was a time of ladies coming together who were in different seasons of their lives. I was able to connect with TJ and the other ladies who attended.

Fast forward, I was going through a season in my life and needed a place to live. I did not know where I was going. We were talking one day, and she welcomed me to stay in their home. As time went on, our bond grew, and she was like a mother to me – God was answering a prayer about a void that was in my life. As time went on, we would talk about the house and what purpose God had for it. On that day, I said to her, "What do you think of *Triumphant Journey* since her initials were TJ." She had this smile on her face. What I did not realize at that this was the name she had in mind. It was a place one could relax, recharge, rejuvenate, refresh, and be reinvented. It was a place to get direction and guidance and to begin finding my way in what I called a wilderness experience in a desert land. This is where my journey started for a reason and in time and a season not knowing what the future held.

DISASTERS

I am going to start off with an excerpt from my journal dated October 14, 2018. I was going through something, and it led me to write this:

STORMS

Sudden Turbulent Opposition Rattling our Mind and Soul

What are storms? When it comes to severe weather, thunderstorms, tornadoes, and hurricanes are regarded as nature's most violent storms. During storms, trees may come down depending on its intensity and power may go out. When the public knows there is a storm alert, i.e., a tornado warning, etc. in the forecast, people run to the stores stocking up on food and supplies.

There always seems to be a storm in the forecast. My question to you is, "What storms have you been in recently? What storm are you currently in – financial, relationship, work, health, family, etc.?" Know this, you are either in a storm, coming out of a storm, or on your way into one. Storms can affect your entire well-being if you allow it. Storms can also go against one's health.

We have had attacks against us that have been huge. Attacks like when there was a high alert about Anthrax, and we had to be careful about opening mail. After that, there were the mail bomb packages that were being left at people's homes and businesses. Now, at the time of my writing, it is the Coronavirus (COVID-19) pandemic that is on the warpath. I call Coronavirus this – **C**allous **O**pposition **R**uining and **O**bstructing as a **N**ational **A**dversary. We must stand on the Word of God and know:

> *"No weapon that formed against thee shall prosper, and every tongue that shall rise against thee in judgment thou shalt condemn. This is the heritage of the Lord, and their righteousness is of me, saith the Lord."* (Isaiah 54.17 KJV)

Then we come to the vicious waves of injustice where my brothers and sisters have been killed suddenly, harshly, without reason and cause. I am reminded as I reflect on Dr. Martin Luther King Jr. speech "We Shall Overcome."

Scriptures

Psalm 107:29 (ESV)

He made the storm be still, and the waves of the seas were hushed.

Matthew 8:23-27 (ESV)

And he got into the boat, his disciples followed him. And behold, there arose a great storm on the sea, so that the boat was being swamped by the waves; but he was asleep. And they went and woke him, saying, "Save us, Lord; we are perishing." And he said to them, "Why are you afraid, O you of little faith?" Then he arose and rebuked the winds and the sea, and there was a great calm. And the men marveled, saying, "What sort of man is this, that even the winds and sea obey him?"

Deuteronomy 31:6 (ESV)

Be strong and courageous. Do not fear or be in dread of them, for it is the Lord your God who goes with you. He will not leave you or forsake you."

Mark 4:35-41 (ESV)

On that day, when evening had come, he said to them, "Let us go across to the other side." And leaving the crowd, they took him with them in the boat, just as he was. And other boats were with him. And a great windstorm arose, and the waves were breaking into the boat, so that the boat was already filling. But he was in the stern, asleep on the cushion. And they woke him said to Him, "Teacher, do you not care that we are perishing?" And he awoke and rebuked the wind and said to the sea, "Peace! Be still!" And the wind ceased, and there was a great calm. He said to them, "Why are you so afraid? Have you still no faith?" And they were filled with great fear and said to one another, "Who then is this, that even the wind and sea obey him?"

When a storm comes, think about palm trees, they have extraordinarily strong roots that create a bottom-heavy base or foundation that helps keep the tree in place – steady. They bend but do not break. They have a swag about them. The life of the palm tree is on the inside. When strong winds come, the palm tree's root system is not weakened but strengthened by the storm. Yes, when the wind blows hard on a palm tree, the roots stretch and grow stronger.

Well, this one morning, as I looked out the bedroom window, it was a beautiful warm, sun shining day, but there was a storm in the forecast. As I watched a palm tree and the winds blowing the leaves to and fro, the trunk just swayed gently. I was fascinated by how it just stood firm and did not seem bothered by it. I am reminded I need to be like that when things come my way by not allowing them to move me or take me off-kilter at times – I need to keep my swag on.

Life Lessons

Strong winds come and go. Difficulties, uncertainty, and stress are a part of life. The difference is made in how we respond to them rather than reacting. It is the way that we work through the storms and who we are after the storm passes that matters most. Instead of feeling defeated, disappointed, and hopeless, let the winds bend, shape, and stretch you and watch yourself grow stronger through it.

With a renewed strength, it will allow you to be resilient and be able to bounce back just like the palm trees. When things get tough, do not give up, do not give in, and do not quit no matter what it looks or feels like.

> *"Surely, he shall deliver thee from the snare of the fowler, and from the noisome pestilence."*
> (Psalm 91:3 KJV)

Stay the course; do not get distracted. Storms come suddenly to get you off course. Trust God, Trust God, Trust God – He will see you through.

As Jeremiah 29:11 says, and I have held on to for a long time,

> *"For I know the plans and thoughts I have for you; says the Lord, plans for peace and well-being and not for disaster to give you a future and a hope."* (AMP)

Even though I held on to this passage of scripture, more times than not, I thought and made my own plans and ended up going nowhere fast and sometimes self-sabotaging my own life. You remember what your mother or father would say? That old saying, "A hard head makes a soft behin." Just like a bee sting, it can hurt, but if you are allergic to it, that is a different story altogether. Like the sting of a bee, you can feel the sting of life.

As you may recall in the *Wizard of Oz,* it started with Dorothy, her family, and the home being swept up by a twister. Before the storm came, it was a clear, beautiful day. It looked to be in the mid-70s. Have you ever heard the saying, the calm before the storm? I believe that was when her journey began.

Have you ever been hit or affected by a natural disaster? Depending on who you to talk to, being faced with a natural disaster will mean different things to different people. Have you ever seen a disaster? Has your life ever felt like a disaster or like one is coming? What is the first thing that comes to your mind when I say disaster? New Jersey's Hurricane Sandy, Louisiana's Hurricane Katrina and Rita, Texas Hurricane Harvey, Texas Hurricane Ike, and no not "Ike and Tina Turner," they all came suddenly and abruptly.

Have you felt like your life was a disaster? Surely, we all have at some time in our life felt the storms, hail, winds, and floods that come in unannounced. I could imagine this is how Dorothy felt when her home was hit by an unexpected storm. The tragedy and chaos that it brings leave you with an insurmountable amount of questions: Where to go? What to do? Who to talk to? When will it be over? Why did this happen to you? How in the world will you get through this?

I had the opportunity to work for the Federal Emergency Management Agency (FEMA) for over thirteen years, providing service to survivors as they recovered through the transition of a natural disaster. I remember working 12 to 14 hours daily 7 days a week for 2 months straight, God gave me the endurance to press, I was fulfilling a purpose. It was more than a job that paid well; it was a ministry to be able to serve others in times of distress, hopelessness, loss, despair, anger, and whatever else they may have been experiencing. I was passionate about what I did, at times going against all protocols because it was not about me and the systems that were in place. It was about doing what God would have me to do. I saw and experienced so much, even though I was not personally affected by those I served. I felt their loss, pain, despair, discouragement, anger, anxiety, and fear – I was them. I thought about how Jesus slept through a storm

I began to search on *YouTube*. I saw this and made this connection you will have to listen to it but here are some lyrics:

Sleep in The Storm by Unspoken

Let the thunder be my comfort
Let the lightning be my guide
Let the waves that rise around me
Hold me gently through the night
For the winds that seem against me
Push me right into Your arms
Teach me how to sleep

There is a scripture that comes to mind when I think of disaster – John 10:10, and it says,

> *"A thief has only one thing in the mind - he comes to steal, slaughter, and destroy. But I have come to give you everything in abundance, more than you expect - Life in its fullness until you overflow."*
> (Passion version)

Have you ever had a marriage, a financial situation, a relationship, work, or whatever that either seems to be in disaster mode or is heading in that direction? Well, I have experienced them all, including my body and health, losing my job, car repossessed, losing housing, estranged relationships, etc. It felt like playing dominoes – you hit one piece, and it only takes one – then everything seems to be affected. Just to give you an example – having to move to Florida from Texas after my last FEMA disaster assignment for Hurricane Harvey had ended and having to stay with my daughter and grandchildren. I found it challenging to obtain employment. After trying over and over to be re-employed with FEMA with truly little success, I had to realize that season of my life had ended.

I even experienced a few disasters in the line of duty. Once I was in a company rental car and was hit by another driver in the rear, and the car had to be towed. Then one day, as I was inspecting the damaged dwelling of one of my applicants, I fell through some boarded flooring and was holding on only by arms. If I did not, I would fall straight through, and there was nothing underneath to hold me up. Lastly, I was infected with MRSA, which almost paralyzed me as it was eating my flesh near my lower spine.

All I can say is that God was with me, keeping me. It is only by His Grace that I am still here. I would say to myself many, many times, "I will live and not die." Now I have only been in Florida for one year, and for the last six months, I thought I was going to lose my mind. God had blessed me with a vehicle while in Texas after my first car was repossessed, due to loss of work and only owing $7,000. Well, anyway, my car was hit (**Picture 1**), and with Florida being a no-fault state, I had to go through my insurance. I had to bite the bullet and pay for the damages to my car even though I was insured. God did bless me to find a vehicle body and collision shop. My car was in there for two weeks, and when I got it back, it looked like it never was in an accident. It was not three weeks later, and my car was hit again, this time by a hospital executive. They took responsibility for the accident, but this time my car was deemed TOTALED (**Picture 2**).

Picture 1 – 1st Accident April 2019

Picture 2 - 2nd Accident May 2019

At this point, I had no car, and their insurance company was only going to give me a pay-out based on the value. Even though the car was deemed totaled, the collision body shop was willing to bring it back to life for the amount for which the insurance company had appraised it for. It was a little over three weeks, the owner himself worked on the car and gave it top priority. I got the car back, and you would have never known that it was totaled. The shop even added a back-up camera system.

Meanwhile, I was experiencing re-occurring pain at the base of head (not from the accidents). After going to the Dr. and getting tests and x-rays they couldn't identify what was going on. The next step was to schedule an appointment with a specialist, but to come to find out my Cobra insurance had just expired. At this point, I am still without employment, and now not able to get the proper medical attention was not an option. As much as I tried to encourage myself about what I was going through, and as they say, the struggle is real. During this time, I recalled something that I heard Sarah Jakes say in one of her messages. She said, "Nothing that you lost has anything to do with where you're going."

The trouble did not stop there. One day my daughter called me crying. She said, "Mom, I got into an accident with your car, and it wasn't my fault." She sobbed deeply while the police officer took the report. She was driving, and again another driver hit my car (**Picture 3**). Thank God my daughter was not killed, hurt, or injured. After sending me the pictures of the car, I had so many mixed emotions. I found myself thinking that I could not afford another financial blow. I had just started a new part-time job in the evenings, and we had access to a rental car, but in my mind, all I could hear was, "What do I do next"? Like I said before, situations will leave you with an insurmountable amount of questions.

Picture 3 – 3rd Accident February 2020

After this accident, the insurance company contacted me to inform me that the settlement would be going directly to the lienholder since I was not the owner. Additionally, I did not have gap insurance, as it was not required in Texas. However, Florida being such an accident-prone state, gap insurance is a necessity, but I did not realize that at the time. I also did not realize that there would be nothing left over and that I would still have to continue to make regular payments.

I was having a melt-down or a breakdown – call it what you may. I cried, I groaned and started to say, "**G**etting **P**retty **S**ick;" of all this craziness - this was my definition of GPS. Now the enemy knew I was at a breaking point, so when I received notice that I would not be getting my tax refund due to owing money I was not aware of, I was done. I felt like Job losing everything, but even in his loss, he still stood strong. The thought of being financially drained, isolated, and my health issues taking its toll on my mind, body, and soul.

My sister, Princess, would call and send me daily messages of encouragement and prayer, letting me know to hold on. She would say there was a reason for what I was going through, that it was part of the journey for the NEXT (in her Caribbean accent). My Mom, T.J., would say "I needed to keep it glued together," and God would not let me go, and that He kept calling my name.

I had to hold on, with the song *God's On Your Side* by the Mississippi Mass Choir, as giving up was not an option because then I would have allowed the devil to win, and I would not have seen the breakthrough on the other side. The test is not just hearing and knowing the Word of God but putting your faith, trust, and belief in God while you are going through it. People would say, "They sure do know how to talk a good game, but can they back it up?" I am going to leave you with this song *Holding On,* by Hezekiah Walker – Better Azusa, The Next Generation 2

So yes, I am without my own vehicle for now. I never thought I would be in this place. As I said, this is just for now. I am believing and trusting everything lost will be RESTORED – a temporary setback for a Major Comeback.

More times than not, you have to tell the storms of life and even get indignant about it and say like the song, *I Told the Storm* by Greg O'Quinn and Joyful Noyze, "When I am weak, He is strong."

As I stated before being intrigued by palm trees – looking at the stature as they stand strong during a storm. It has a deep-rooted foundation; it represents a substance of strength, and I want to be like that palm tree that is not moved by the trials and tests of life. As the word of God, being my firm foundation says in Psalm 1:3,

And he shall be like a tree planted by the rivers of water, that bringeth forth his fruit in his season; his leaf shall not wither; and whatsoever he doeth shall prosper. (KJV)

In Isaiah 40, He says,

But those who wait on the Lord, Shall renew their strength; They shall mount up with wings like eagles, They shall run and not be weary, They shall walk and not faint. NKJV

I was reminded hearing this from a message I heard, did you know that when a storm approaches, an eagle uses the storm to his advantage? When the eagle flies toward the storm, he fixes his wings a certain way, and the wind takes him higher flying above the storm. Sometimes, in all honesty, I have found it easier said than done. I am still a working progress, having to learn to spread my wings so I can fly above the storms of life.

One of the songs that ministered to me and that I would sing during the times of storms and trials of life is:

My Soul Is Anchored by Douglas Miller
From the Album: ***Unspeakable Joy***

But if the storms don't cease, and if the winds keep on blowing in my Life.
My soul has been anchored in the Lord.
I realize that sometimes in this Life, we're gonna be tossed.
By the waves and the currents that seems so fierce.
But in the word of God, I got an anchor.
And it keeps me steadfast, unmovable, despite the tides!

It has brought me through on numerous occasions, giving me a sense of going somewhere over the rainbow. You know, like where Dorothy ends up after her disaster? She finds herself going to that place that she had sung about, *Somewhere Over the Rainbow*.

My Testimony by Marvin Sapp

So glad I made it,
I made it through
In spite of the storm and rain, heartache, and pain
I'm still alive declaring you I made it through See, I didn't lose.
Experience lost at a major cost

The place where Dorothy ends up is a place of paradise. I will call it a *DEEP Oasis*. It is a place you can only imagine – where birds chirp, beautiful flowers blossom, and sounds of water streaming. A place so serene, so scenic – it is breathtaking (get a picture in your mind). Have you ever seen or visited such a place? So, let us go to the DEEP Oasis for a while.

DEEP Oasis

The name DEEP Oasis originated shortly after *Triumphant Journey* came into being. DEEP Oasis was a place one could go to be refreshed, renewed, restored, and reinvented or you can say, "Relax, Relate, and Release." A place where one could go to meditate, reinventing from a DEEP place, not just examining surface issues, but its root. Again, it is about going DEEP – a time of transparency.

Dorothy's family told her that she needed to "Find a place where you won't get into any trouble far, far away." This is when she sings, *Somewhere over the Rainbow*. Depending on who you were telling this to today, it might not be taken too well, to say the least. Dorothy and Toto end up in place of paradise (*Paradise* by Norman Brown). It is a beautiful place of flawless blue skies, sounds of nature, birds are chirping and tweeting, flowers of every color of the rainbow, green pastures, the serenity of the springs, and palm trees dancing in the breeze. Again, the palm tree does not just represent the substance of strength but also of a scene in nature as in Ezekiel 41:23-26 where it says,

> *Both the main Sanctuary and the Holy Place had double doors. Each door had two leaves; two leaves for each door, one set swinging inward, and the other set outward. The doors of the main Sanctuary were carved with angel-cherubim and palm trees. There was a canopy of wood in front of the vestibule outside. There were narrow windows alternating with carved palm trees on both sides of the porch.* (MSG)

Your DEEP Oasis might be one of our many beautiful Islands. A resort you could go to and look onto the heavenly skies and say, "What a mighty God I serve, look at what He has created."

Dorothy and Toto are in a foreign land, and she did not know that it was going to be a faith journey - step by step,

> *For we walk by faith and not by sight.* 2 Corinthians 5:7 NIV

Have I not commanded you? Be strong and courageous,

"Do not be afraid; do not be discouraged, for the Lord your God will be with you wherever you go."
Joshua 1:9 NIV

Now when they arrived at that place called "There," besides the beauty, it was a city where the munchkins lived. By Dorothy's house landing forcibly on the ground, it fell on top of the Wicked Witch of the West, so she could no longer harass them. They were excited, happy, and free to live without living in bondage, as this was originally a happy place with happy people. Dorothy had become their angel in disguise, and they were ready to celebrate. They were able to live in peace and enjoy God's beautiful creation. This is also where Dorothy gets the ruby slippers that the Wicked Witch of the West wore.

The ruby slippers represented one's ability to triumph over powerful forces. It is a stone of nobility and considered the most magnificent of all gems - the queen of stones and the stone of kings. It is also said that rubies have an intense inner power that can give you the strength to take risks and try new things. Does this not sound like reinventing and renovations? I will be touching more on this a little later. Sometimes along the journey, you will lose your way but, thank God, He is the One who can restore and put us back together again.

This is the song they were singing when they woke up to the start of the morning. Now you know I have a song so sing along:

"Good Morning" by Mandisa

Wave away my yesterday Cause I'm leaving it behind me. Hello sunshine
come what may. I feel something new inside me…..

Wake up to a brand-new day

JOURNEY ROAD – EMERALD CITY

Within your heart you can make plans for your future,
But the Lord chooses the step you take to get there. Proverbs 16:9 (TPT)

Dorothy is on her journey, walking along the way to Emerald City to see the Wizard as you should know by now, the song is *Take Me to The King*. She was probably walking down roads and going through fields. Well, we are going to bring it to the present day. I might be cruising along in the car, walking, or I might be on a flight to some destination. How are you traveling? Have you ever been on a trip that you thought was a short distance, but once you got started, it took longer than you thought? The GPS says, for example, "4 hours and 24 minutes," but it takes seven hours instead, or even longer. Did you make some stops along the way, was there an accident, traffic jam, sightseeing, speed limits? Bottom line, it took longer than you expected without a doubt.

The road during your journey will have a lot of twists and turns, sometimes suddenly unknown curves. (order my steps).

Now, I will have some headphones on listening to my music as I am walking – maybe listening to *I'm Every Woman Radio* on Pandora. Walking in step with music, singing, moving to the beat of the music, in my own little world, people driving by likely saying, "Look at her." Sometimes they even beeped with a thumbs up.

There are also times when we may run off the road onto the curb or even a ditch. Sometimes the car might have some mechanical issues causing it to stall, and not sure if it will start again needing maintenance along the way (roadside service). There are times when you had to take an alternative route - you will get there but not how you planned, so you ask the question, "Which direction do I go?" Not Sure? Thank God for those GPS systems, but even sometimes they can go haywire. However, to answer that question, God gives us insight and direction to follow the paths He has for us having an ear to hear what He is saying. "He is not going to show us the entire way from the beginning - just one step at a time as we need it," as Dr. Charles Stanley would say. Proverb 3:5 says

Trust in the Lord with all your heart and do not lean on your own understanding; in all your ways submit to Him, and He will make your paths straight. NIV

Think about the choices you make because CHOICES = CONSEQUENCES? Jeremiah 29:13-14 says this,

> *You will seek me and find me when you seek me with your heart. I will be found by you," declares the Lord, "and will bring you back from captivity. I will gather you from all the nations and places where I have banished you," declares the Lord, "and will bring you back to the place from which I carried into exile.* NIV

As I have reflected on my own life, there were many times I have taken a path based on feelings and emotions moving too fast, and then it all backfires. As you get older and wiser, you must slow it down and think about what you are thinking about. You cannot make microwave decisions; they must cook and sometimes put in a crockpot for a slow simmer. Also, along the way, you will have many voices talking to you physically and mentally – advising that you should do this, and you should do that. You find out everyone has an opinion on what they think is best for you; the reality is there is only One who knows what is best for you, and that is Jesus. When you listen to what everybody has to say, as my Mom TJ would say, "Sometimes our thinking and thoughts are like scrambled eggs."

Now, do not get me wrong. There is nothing wrong with seeking advice from your trusted friend or family member. How one person may handle something, or their perspective may be different from how you are directed to go. You cannot make them wrong to make you right, and you cannot make you right to make them wrong. Sometimes you must be still and wait on God – by the way, I have a song, *I Don't Mind Waiting* by Juanita Bynum. I believe that is where my anxiety and anxiousness would flare up because I could not wait on God; I had a panic button.

I said before, you would see that I use different songs with their lyrics as I see Dorothy,

Scarecrow, Tinman, and the Lion sang as they walked down the road to see the Wizard (*Take Me to The King*). They sang to each other since they walked a lot. On the other hand, me and the crew would be in the car or even walking singing this song by Mariah Carey.

Hero

There's a hero
If you look inside your heart
You don't have to be afraid
Of what you are
There's an answer

It is a Saturday morning after the totaling of my car; I was walking to the local library to do some writing and schoolwork, as it had become a routine anyway – part of staying fit and fabulous. As I am walking, it is a little cool outside, just enough to need a long sleeve sweater, remember I am in Florida right now. I have my headphones on listening to Gospel music and singing, praising God, focusing, and keeping my mind on Him. It came to my remembrance; I am in the same place (season) but a different location physically from where I was when staying at the top of the hill in Apalachin, NY, where my journey started. I was in a place of transition where we have all been at some time or another. Like a road, life had taken me through various twists and turns – losing the first car I owned and waiting on employment opportunities.

While residing in Apalachin, I felt isolated as I lived outside the city, and there were no buses that traveled this road. I was not able to use my cell phone due to poor service connection. The best way to be reached was by landline. Since the service connection was poor, I had to go down toward the bottom of the hill to check to see if anyone contacted me or left any messages that I needed to return or follow up on. The flip side was, I was being courted (old school term) by a man from the church I attended. When he found out about my car, he would drive at least twice a day to take me where I needed to go or just to see me. Now let me tell you, this was a rugged, long road, and I did not live around the corner from where he lived, but he was faithful and committed. To fast forward, we did end up getting married. So, you see, there were bitter and sweet moments, hard and easy, smooth, and rough times.

While now residing in Florida, my life felt like it had gone full circle again. I was back to seeking full-time employment, as I was working part-time in the evenings, divorced, dealing with the loss of a vehicle, and feeling isolated. I was in a place where I had not developed friendships per se and had no potential male friendships or relationship. My new road has me enrolled at the University of Phoenix in an online program for a Bachelor of Science in Public Administration degree, where I have by the grace of God been nominated for the "National Society of Collegiate Scholars and National Society of Leadership and Success." I am writing my first book project that I never thought in a million years would happen. God has strengthened my bond with my sister, Princess (feeling like my natural one), seeing my grandchildren grow, and restoring the relationship with my daughter. There has been growth in areas of my life that needed to be matured. Regardless of everything that is happening right now, He has taken me down another road – it has been an adventure, to say the least.

Then I thought why the name Emerald City. It could have been called any other name. Why Emerald? The emerald, according to jewelry notes, "conveys a more complex set of symbolism and emotions, by nature is the most calming of all the colors, it also encourages growth, reflection, peace and balance as well as healing and fertility." That's when it all came together. It was an A-ha moment. Along this journey road, I have met people who were for a reason, season, and some for a lifetime. You will get a chance to know some of them as you go along with me on my journey. While I am going on mine, think about those that have come across your path whether it was for a reason, season, or lifetime – Journey Travelers.

JOURNEY TRAVELERS

Before we get to the story of Dorothy and her crew, my question to you is, who is your crew? Who do you surround yourself with? Who are your influencers? Does your crew consist of any of the characters in Dorothy's life? Now, before you answer those questions, think about it for a minute or two. Does your crew consist of Social Media and Facebook followers – those you do not know? What about your cell phone? We have our cell phone with us 24/7/365 with all our contacts and messaging platforms (Facebook, Messenger, Twitter, Periscope, etc.). Every time I turn around, there is another app to download to be connected to someone or something! We can even get messages through a smartwatch that is smarter than you. I came from back in the day of having to turn the channel when there was no such thing as a remote. Now we have ROKU, Smart TV, Netflix; we do not need anything else. Now do not get me wrong they are nice to have, but sometimes they are used as distractions – there must be balance. Now Dorothy's crew, along with Toto of course, are a mixed bunch.

First comes across the Scarecrow who desires a **BRAIN.**

As they continue along their journey to Emerald City, they cross paths with the Tinman who desires

HEART.

Lastly, they run into the Cowardly Lion, who desires **COURAGE.** The Cowardly Lion believes that his fear makes him inadequate and desires COURAGE. He makes a statement, "*I'm afraid there's no denying, I'm just a Dandy Lion, a fate I don't deserve! But I could show my prowess, be a lion, not a mouse, if I only had the Nerve.*"

I am quite sure that he wished he sounded like the Lion that roars at the beginning of the movie. They all really needed each other, they were part of a puzzle, and each one of them played a significant role in making the picture whole.

I have felt like the Cowardly Lion many times truth be told. I believe that it has stemmed from low self-esteem and confidence. This is something that I have had to work through once I acknowledged it. I had a lot going for me, but I had feelings of not being good enough, comparing myself to others, and looking for others' approval. Have you ever felt like that at one time or another? I have also been like the Tinman by not using the good sense that God gave me, not making good or wise choices. Let me tell you it is like having a good thing, and you think it is sweeter on the other side, allowing your flesh and emotions to get in the way, saying goodbye and letting it go. It is having foolish thinking going on, thinking you know what is better for you than what God has for you (reality check). Then when it comes to the Scarecrow, allowing hurt and disappointment not just in other people but for myself sometimes feeling the hollowness of heart. If you did not know, you are more than enough, you were created in the image of God as Psalm 139:14 NIV says,

I praise you because I am fearfully and wonderfully made; your works are wonderful, I know that full well.

You must believe that!!!

Do you have any fears? Or are you in need of more courage in one or more areas? Now tell the truth. In going back to school in my later years, I was hesitant and a little fearful, but on the other hand, it was something I wanted to accomplish. It was a goal of mine for a long time, and now was the time. Well, I went back, and with some anxiety, let me tell you, once I did make up my mind to do it, there were more distractions coming at me – medical issues attacking my body, financial issues, it seemed like it was one thing right after another. I know the devil thought I would not go through with and give in, but he didn't know who he was dealing with. I was determined and focused on achieving my goal, and failure was not an option. Let me tell you I ended up doing better than I ever thought I would have. Yes, I had to do the hard work, but God was with me the whole time and as they say, that is "Keeping It Real!"

I can do all things through Christ who strengthens me. (Philippians 4:13 NKJV)

I am a witness.

Not by might nor by power, but by my Spirit. (Zechariah 4:6 KJV)

It has been said, "Some people come into your life for a reason, a season or a lifetime."

Sometimes the biggest thing is to know which one it is – you must be discerning. You also must know when to Scroll, Select, and Delete from that LONG list you have. Everybody who Dorothy met along her journey to Emerald City was significant; there was a purpose. Sometimes we do not why people come briefly like a thief in the night, but later, you come to realize there was a reason and then you have one of those A-HA moments. Now you know the Scarecrow, Tinman, and the Lion were all her family members just dressed or illustrating another character. Remember, in the beginning, one of her uncles (Hunk) was telling her about staying out of trouble, but then he went on to say, "Need to use your brains and well your head is not made of straw, you know." Her other uncle says to her, "Have a little courage, I would spit in her eye that is what I would do!" I wonder deep down inside if that was how they were feeling? Just a thought.

We play different characters from time to time like Jekyll and Hyde, Good Girl and Bad Girl, Good Boy and Bad Boy, and sometimes you feel like a nut, and sometimes you don't. So, who have you come across in your travels? I had never thought about it, but everyone who has come across my path was for a reason, whether it was for a minute or two. I remember times when I would go into a grocery or retail store and end up just talking to a stranger out of the clear blue sky. I might have had a rough day, or she might have, but I left different saying, "Wow."

There have been many travelers who have come across my path who have made me reflect on many things from time to time as part of my education in life. While living in my hometown of Binghamton, NY, a friend worked at the local electric and gas company as a Customer Service Representative. When I would pay my utility bill, I never paid attention to the fact he had ducks inside of his window where he served the customers. Each time I would go in, I would notice more and more ducks of all different sizes, shapes, and even some in different colors. Well, one day I went to pay my bill; it was not busy at the time, and there were no lines, so I asked the usual questions about how his day was going, just small talk. Then I asked him about all the ducks. Why so many? Why ducks? I remember him talking about how his job entails working with the public, and sometimes people can be not so nice or friendly. He explained to me that ducks have an oil finish on them, and that is why water rolls right off them. He goes on to explain, you must learn how to sometimes let what people say just roll off you like the water on the duck – respond not react. The next time I went to pay my bill, I brought him a soft fluffy duck. This has stayed with me for many years, and even today, I have had to learn and still keep in my remembrance to let what people say roll off of me or let it go because it is not hurting them; it is hurting you.

Remember - Let it roll; let it roll!

After many years, I was able to reconnect informing him of my book project and how what he said about ducks stayed with me for so many years. He stated after he retired, taking all his ducks with him, and the one I gave him, he called her Grace – for God's Grace.

When I was in Texas, the church I attended the Pastors walked in anointing and authenticity and made an impact in my life. When I started attending, I was amid a lot of transition and did not know what to do in different instances. They encouraged, empowered, and supported me during a critical time, and I will never forget it. In times of altar call, I would go up for prayer, and she would always say to me, "God's Got You," give me a hug and smile. When he preached, it was like he was speaking directly to me - God used him as a voice speaking life to what was dying inside me.

I left Texas and went to Charleston, South Carolina, due to loss of employment and had faced financial difficulties. This is where my car was repossessed. While I was in Charleston, I lived down the street from a nearby church. One day as I was walking, I stopped by the church office building. While there, I was introduced to the Pastor's wife. She was the food pantry Director who assisted the community with not only food but also other resources. I had the opportunity to be her Assistant.

While assisting her, the Pastor invited me to attend the executive staff meetings. I was honored since I was only a volunteer. I was able to watch as he conducted business, doing everything in excellence. He valued the staff who worked for him. He would tell me to smile all the time as I would carry a serious demeanor upon my face. When I was working on a project and so happened to pass him walking to the office, he would say, "Pick your head up and smile." I really did appreciate it, him telling me made me think and to discipline myself in the area. He was not only a Pastor but a businessman and entrepreneur. The Pastor, and his wife had a restaurant, and they had the best chicken wings!

I then obtained a job assignment in Austin, Texas. While there, I was seeking a church when I came across The House of Intercession (THOI), located on Delmar Ave., whose pastor is Eric D. White Sr. I felt that was where I was led to go, the street was the name of my spiritual father – Mr. Delma R. West where *Triumphant Journey* began. I remember the Sunday morning I entered the church; it felt like I was there before, my spirit was revived. I cannot even explain all that happened in that service. I continued to worship there until my job assignment was over and even when over, I still stayed connected with some of the members I met. When I was no longer there, I would watch the services through Eric D. White Sr., Periscope (social media platform), which at that time, I had never heard of it. The Pastor shared in July 2019 he felt led to do, "30 Ways For 30 Days." He worked for the postal service, and during his lunch breaks, he would log on to Periscope and deliver a different message each day. Each was so anointed and appointed in that season. I would get my journal out and write notes to reflect on and sometimes share with others, just to give you a taste:

Day #1 "Being Well with His Will" in short - "We can't always trace His will but we must TRUST it, the very will for our lives."

Day #4 "The Trip Was Worth the Trouble" - in short, "God has so many discoveries He wants to show us so don't worry about arriving to your destination."

In one of his messages he used the illustration from *The Wizard of Oz*. Now, writing a book at that time was not a thought plus *The Wizard of Oz* as a theme. And now fast forward writing a book and using it as a theme – again NEVER would have thought it. Wow

Each one of them were apostolic and visionary men and women of God! Now, they are not the only ones that I have met along the way; some of my travelers have turned out to be my closest friends. You must know there is a difference between confidants, acquaintances, and friends. How do you distinguish them? I have, at times, made the mistake of not being able to distinguish between them. What kind of friend would you say you are? In asking myself that question, I have not been or acted like a good friend to some of my friends - I mean real friends. I have had to go back and apologize and get it right. Reflecting over your life, you will realize the many people that have crossed your path, and you would be amazed. Now that we have encountered the different people along the way, let us view things from a different perspective in how it resulted in us being reinvented or renovations made in us.

R.E.N.O.V.A.T.I.O.N.S

Re-inventing **E**verything **N**ecessary **of** **V**ulnerable **A**ttachments **T**ransforming **i**nto **N**ew **S**urprises

On Dorothy's way to Emerald City to see the Wizard (the King of Kings), she was being transformed and reinvented in a way that would change her life forever. Even though Dorothy looked manicured on the outside, there were things, like you and me, that needed some attention (I use that word attention). She had a fear factor like standing up for herself when it came to Miss Gulch, who wanted to take Toto from her and would chase her down the road. She was smart, but I think she was intimidated so she would not respond back. If you think about it, everyone who she encountered along the way was being reinvented and transformed (Scarecrow, Tin Man, Lion), and they were there for each other, I do not think they realized it at that moment.

God wanted to restore the roar of the Lion representing royalty and kingship. For the Scarecrow, He wanted to restore thoughts to the mindless and the Tin Man restoring a heart to the heartless.

Before I go any further, what areas in your life need to be reinvented? According to the *Cambridge Dictionary*: reinvent means to produce something new that is based on something that already exists. Then I looked up the meaning of renovations. *Merriam-Webster* says it this way; renew, restore, refresh, renovate, rejuvenate mean to make like new, renew implies a restoration of what had become a faded or disintegrated so that it seems like new.

Have you ever started to do some renovations in your house because it needed some improvements or just wanted to change what was old to something newer? If so, you know it can be a time of discomfort and chaos from everything in being in disarray.

I received a call from an old Boo from a long time ago, and he said hello, "Butterfly." That was the name that he gave me when we first met. I remember a book that he gave me that contained dozens of butterfly graphics. During that time, I thought it was sweet, but I had not captured the true meaning of a butterfly. Now looking back over twenty years plus years, I can see how God had put me through a metamorphosis going through everything I had to go through to become the person that He wanted me to become for His distinct purpose and His perfect will. The process of going through the different stages of life and development gave me a whole new perspective. Did you realize that during the metamorphosis stage from caterpillar to becoming a butterfly, one part is dying so the other can come alive? We must die in some areas, so the revealing of the new can come forth. I will share something he said, "I understand some things about butterflies today, that I didn't always know. You can't capture a butterfly and make it your own; you have to give it the freedom to fly; it only visits if it wants to, and no two butterflies are the same."

On Netflix, there is a series called *Designated Survivor*. When I started to look at it, I thought it was just another show to look at, but it took on a completely different perspective. I saw it in a totally different light. The main actor (Kirkland) was being reinvented and had to stand strong in the face of opposition, not knowing who was really on his side (watching, discerning). Here is a little bit about the story; it is about the HUD Housing Secretary (Kirkland), who works for the President of the United States of America. He is called into the office to be informed he will no longer holds the position he was in - he is being fired and placed into another position. Mr. Kirkland cannot understand why he is being removed when so much progress had been made; he had found purpose in what he was doing.

Not too soon after this, Mr. Kirkland receives a call asking to fill the position of the Designated Survivor, meanwhile, there is an explosion in the Capitol. Mr. Kirkland is sent to the scene, and as he is being transported, top Security informs Mr. Kirkland that the President is dead, and being the Designated Survivor, he has been appointed to fill the position of President (this takes him completely off guard, he is stunned!). Mr. Kirkland is sworn in as the President. He then goes to the Men's Restroom into a stall and just stands there thinking about what just had happened, embracing the fact he has been appointed, and sick to his stomach. Meanwhile, the Speaker of the House is in the stall next to him in nervousness of what is happening and says, "I don't know how Mr. Kirkland got appointed out of all the others who would be more qualified." The government staff is disappointed with the selection and does not feel Mr. Kirkland can do the job. Mr. Kirkland starts to question his ability to carry out such an appointment, he does not have the necessary degrees or experience. As decisions must be made, other high-ranking staff members conspire against him since they feel he is inadequate for the position. Mr. Kirkland, now as the appointed President, had to face many challenges, trials, opposition, and even himself and his family (wife, daughter, and son). Toward the end of the series, he finds out who he thought at that time informed him the United States President was not him someone else disguised as him called. He was not qualified but CHOSEN.

You see, man did not put him in position, but GOD did. While in the Presidency, he had to become stronger and wiser. His staff began to respect the man in the position; they were proud to serve under his direction. He had integrity, character, and did the right thing when nobody else agreed. He continued to face heightened challenges and battles (David & Goliath) more than he thought he could handle, but you will see God went before him, protected him. He also had to face the death of his wife of many years, even though a part of him died with her he had to stand strong in being there for his daughter and son. During the same time, God restored his relationship with his brother; it was like death on one side and life on the other. In man's eyes, you may not be qualified but CHOSEN by God.

Some things I have taken away from watching the show - Life Lessons:

1. He had to walk and talk with confidence despite his fears.

2. No weapon formed against you shall prosper.

3. He could not waver he had to take a stand for what was right.

4. He did and would not compromise his values.

5. Always had to be professional in the way he presented himself even though he was tempted to do otherwise.

6. God will open doors and opportunities that you never saw coming.

7. Do not let anyone take your POWER away from you.

8. Do not let others dictate to you or control/undermine you.

9. Do not let others define who you are - everyone has an opinion.

10. Know that you know God has chosen you for the position (others might not think you are qualified - experience, education, knowledge), but it does not matter.

11. Everyone does not want you to succeed.

12. Watch and be aware (discerning) of people's motives.

13. You will feel overwhelmed and not sure which direction to go in - "*Trust in the Lord, with all thy heart lean not unto your own understanding but acknowledge Him and He shall direct thy path.*" Proverbs 3:5-6

14. Be STRONG and Be of Good COURAGE.

15. When and where I am weak, He is strong.

16. Lead like a lion.

17. You will be mocked.

18. Maintain your composure - Don't let them see you sweat.

19. Do not get distracted by the naysayers in life.

20. Respond; do not react.

21. Know who you are and whose you are.

22. Do not let others determine your confidence or self-esteem.

23. The importance of having a supportive family to encourage you no matter what.

24. Pray without ceasing.

25. Trust God - seek His guidance not man's.

26. Be careful who you have in your inner circle - Scroll, Select, Delete!

27. Everybody that smiles in your face is not always for you but trying to obtain information.

"Old things have passed away – behold, all things have become new." 2 Corinthians 5:17 (KJV)

Now my question is, has God ever had to reinvent or renovate your house, Meaning YOU? Are you currently undergoing a renovation? I am just saying; I believe God has had and may still be doing some renovations. In this season of my life, I have been under some MAJOR reinventing and renovations. It has been the most isolating, challenging, frustrating and uncomfortable times in my life the song, *He's Preparing Me* by Daryl Coley (extended version). I thought as I was older, it would not seem so intense, but who am I? It took some time to understand that what God had purposed in my life was more than I could see, and some things needed attention in preparation according to His purpose and plan for my life the song; *My Life is Not My Own* by William McDowell As God has continually reminded me of Jeremiah 29:11,

"For I know the plans I have for you, declares the LORD, plans to prosper you and not to harm you, plans to give you hope and a future." (NIV)

All of us at some point in time or another, some minor and then some major renovations have had to be made. In the shaping, this is…

> *This is the word that came to Jeremiah from the LORD: "Go down to the potter's, and there I will give you my message." So, I went down to the potter's house, and I saw him working at the wheel. But the pot he was shaping from the clay was marred in his hands; so the potter formed it into another pot, shaping it as seemed best to him.* Jeremiah 18 (NIV)

Usually, before you start any renovation, let's say project (I love projects), you need to know what areas you are focusing on determining who needs to assist you, who you need to hire or if you can do it yourself. There is also the fact of how much is this going to cost (need a financial plan) to pay somebody else for their services, or how much time you have yourself to invest? Projects have a **PROCESS,** and sometimes the pain of the process feels like you are being crushed, it feels unbearable. Sometimes I cry because the crushing is so intense, but I know it had to be done to see the other side. God says, "All things work together for good," but sometimes during the process it does not feel like that at that time. I know I have felt like saying and have said, "God can we skip over this part or just review this part or section because going through may take some time," Then He reminds me of **TIME;** You know God has a sense of humor because I said TIME – Tick, Tock. He goes well, "I made the *TICK and the TOCK of* TIME (Shut my Mouth).

Ecclesiastes 3:1-8 (KJV)

> *"To everything there is a season, and a time to every purpose under the Heaven: A time to be born, and a time to die; a time to plant, and a time to pluck up that which is planted; A time to kill, and a time to heal; a time to break down, and a time to build up; A time to weep, and a time to laugh; a time to mourn, and a time to dance; A time to cast away stones, and a time to gather stones together; a time to embrace, and a time to refrain from embracing; A time to get, and a time to lose; a time to keep, and a time to cast away; A time to rend, and a time to sew; a time to keep silence, and a time to speak; A time to love, and a time to hate; a time of war, and a time of peace."*

At this point I come to my senses and say, "Okay, God, we might as well get started (hesitantly); the sooner I learn what I need to learn, the sooner we can move to the next step." You know He already knows what you think anyway, so you might as well put it out there. I am also reminded many times over and over of something a friend would say, "In the Fullness of Time," the song *He Knows My Name,* Tasha Cobbs Leonard – Jimi Cravity.

Renovating can be hard work and sometimes painful – sometimes it goes **DEEP;** not just surface stuff, things we have been carrying, things that we thought was the truth but are really lies that the devil planted in our heads or our ways of thinking. You might think about doing some outside renovating planting some flowers, trees, landscaping, but those are external fashions. It is like adding accessories to your outfit like some jewelry that has bling. The outside is easy, you can even throw a cute hat on, but the core the internal that is where the real beauty lies. You know those selfies you take – how many do you take of yourself? The question of who you really are under all those selfies because you know you can alter the picture where it can look like a photographer professionally took it.

Sometimes the surfaces had to be scrubbed down to wipe away small particles, residue, and dust that surfaces. Sometimes God has to do some DEEP cleansing within the crevices of our soul and heart, cleansing away and through those DEEP places where hurt, shame, disappointment, and even self-sabotaging ways we have done to our self that has had us bond (in bondage). Just like renovations, the reinventing of oneself is real! You have heard, and I have said it before, "The Struggle Is Real."

Sometimes walls had to be torn down, demolishing the comfortable places to an uncomfortable place – looking at yourself in the mirror with no makeup. There are those stubborn stains you know what they say, "Shout it Out!" Like my Mom, T.J., would say to me a lot of times, "Sometimes, you have to spank your own self on your hands." Now that can be hurtful, especially if you have heavy hands! Also, sometimes looking at yourself and saying I am a "HOT MESS," do you say how is anything good going to come out of this? YES, because,

> And we know that all things work together for good to those who love God, to those who are called according to His purpose" Romans 8:28 NKJV

and

> For we walk by faith and not by sight. 2 Corinthians 5:7 NIV

God wants us to be whole on the inside out, not on the outside in. In one of my readings, it was put this way,

> It speaks from the lens of divine wisdom. That is deep in our hearts has the capacity to show up in our lives, no matter how you have attempted to create your own presentation.

So, what are you holding onto in your heart that allows the process of being reinvented halted by placing a stop sign in your journey rather than the green light?

Surface stuff is superficial, but that inward man is where the renovation counts. Have you seen those shows like *Flip That House* where people come in and do a complete makeover? Everything is torn up from the floor up. You watch them; they are strategic, and God is strategic with us as well. Now, remember the house that they are working on; the people who live there are not there while the work is being completed. Well, that is how God is with us, He will come in and do some extensive renovation work. Now, He will not go against your will, if you want to stay the way you are, I always use the term "Hot Mess." Then what can I say, and who am I? Let me tell you I am an ongoing project.

On the other hand, if you want to live a purposeful life wanting to be what God has purposed you to be, then you will have to go through the PROCESS. Tamela Mann sings the song *Change Me*. Well, back to what I was saying when the house is finished, you cannot even recognize it, you think you are going to someone's house. God can do a renovation that when He gets done, people will notice, and you will not even have to say anything. God will sometimes isolate you so that He can do a DEEP work in and through you. There will be such light reflected as they say, "I Once Was Blind, but Now I See." You can put a price on man's renovations, but when God does a renovation, it is PRICELESS.

During a new part-time job training (onboarding), one of the videos was "Emotional Intelligence," something I had not experienced as part of a training. Still, it made me reflect on how it associated itself with the reinventing and renovation process. The key points in "Emotional Intelligence" are first, KNOW YOURSELF (what makes you unique), secondly, CHOOSE YOURSELF (managing your thoughts, feelings, actions, and emotions) and finally, BE YOURSELF (is when you know yourself and choose yourself). After looking at the video, I said to myself, "Wow!" Psalm 51:10 says,

Create in me a clean heart, O God, And renew a steadfast right spirit within me. NKJV

Another one of my songs, *Deliver Me (This Is My Exodus)* by Donald Lawrence and Le'andria Johnson.

Think about where you are, reflecting on the characters and where you might have to reinvent yourself in some areas? (food for thought)

Scarecrow

1. What areas do you feel inadequate in?
2. Where do you go when lacking faith?
3. How do you see yourself?
4. Why do you feel the way you do?
5. Who has affected the ways you feel?

Cowardly Lion

1. Who are you afraid of?
2. What are the fears that are keeping you away from moving forward?
3. Where is your courage lacking?
4. Why are you fearful?
5. How do you overcome?

Tin Man

1. What areas in your heart have you harden yourself in?

2. Where have you lost your joy in?

3. What people or things affect the way you feel?

4. Why do you allow those things to affect you?

5. How do you cope with your feelings?

Larnell Harris and James Fortune remind me I can begin and dream again.

I Can Begin Again by Larnell Harris.

Deep into the Father's eyes
And see that there is hope for one like me
I can begin again
With the passion of a child
My heart has caught a vision
Of a life that's still worthwhile

Dream Again by James Fortune and Todd Galberth

This is not the end of your story
(*It's a new season*)
Turn the page, prepare for His glory
It's your moment,
You should own it (right now)
The time is now

Dorothy is no longer the same person; she may be in the physical, but so much has changed about her on the inside out. As she comes to the end of her journey, and now looking back, so let us see how her way of thinking became triumphant.

TRIUMPHANT

The meaning of triumphant, according to *Merriam-Webster Dictionary,* means victorious, conquering triumphant armies and rejoicing for or celebrating victory a triumphant shout. In Psalm 47:1, it says,

O clap your hands, all ye people; shout unto God with the voice of triumph. KJV

Our opinion of triumphant is not God's opinion of triumphant. When He says,

For my thoughts are not your thoughts, neither are your ways my ways. Isaiah 55 NIV

I think of Dr. Martin Luther King Jr., Nelson Mandela, Rosa Parks, and there are so many, many others. Then I think about Steve Harvey, Tyler Perry, T.D. Jakes, Les Brown, Oprah Winfrey; there are just so many others I could name. The scripture that comes to my mind is Zechariah 4:10 NIV when it says,

Who dares despise the day of small beginnings.

As the song goes, *We Fall Down* by Donnie McClurkin, there have been many times I have fallen, and sometimes it felt like an airplane that crashed. It is one thing to hit rock bottom it's another thing to getting back up, so I have learned not to be so critical and judgmental based on anyone's past and even present because we all have one time, or another has fallen. We all have a history and yours is no worse than mine and mine no worse than yours. As Princess would say instead of judging just say, "They are just expressing themselves."

We must look past what you know and look at what you see now and say, "I have changed despite what you think. I think of my life, the places, people, and things along the way that brought me to where I am now everything played a part when I think it was strategic, nothing just happened."

Maya Angelou (April 4, 1928, to May 28, 2014) and her poem *Phenomenal Woman,* but most of all, one of my favorites of her quotes, "Wouldn't Take Nothing for My Journey." It also takes me back to our forefathers (ancestors) before us and the journey they lived, leaving us individually a family legacy that was triumphant despite everything they went through. There is another quote, "Thus, out of small beginnings greater things have been produced by His hand that made all things of nothing and gives being to all things that are; and, as one small candle may light a thousand, so the light here kindled hath shone unto many…." (Bradford, William).

When I look and reflect on my life, there have been, still is and will continue to be, many triumphant moments, like when I told you at the beginning where I had moved to Florida and staying with my daughter and grandchildren. I really wanted a place to call of my own, but circumstances did not allow for that. It was where God wanted me to be, as myself and daughter had an estranged relationship. Through us living in the same house, God healed what was broken and restored us in having a mother and daughter relationship that only God could do. He is the RESTORER of what is broken.

Remember when I told you about my car that I no longer have? Well, as I told you, I wasn't working except for a part-time job, I still had car payments, car insurance, cell phone, and internet bills. My children supported and assisted me financially, making sure everything was paid monthly they were there for me, with no grumbling or complaining and never made me feel like a burden to them as the song goes, *Great Is Your Mercy* (Live) by Donnie McClurkin and Travis Greene singing *He Made A Way* – singing along with them with a thankful heart.

Remember, I celebrated my birthday in January, had no idea not even in the realm of my thinking that I would be residing in Maryland right now. It was exactly four months to the day that I relocated to Maryland, but God made a way, and I am looking forward to seeing what God has in store. I am like the butterfly who is coming out of the cocoon. God was and is my Provider, my Protector, my Healer, and my Restorer - He is a Waymaker and Miracle Worker, I am a witness!

Remember, I told you about my tax refund, well I received a letter stating it was an error that my last employer had made and that they were going to refund all the money back to me – Look at God!

I thank God for bringing me into a new year, new decade, and a new season doing a new Thing. As Isaiah 43:18-19 (Passion Translation) says,

> *Stop dwelling of the past. Don't even remember these former things.*
>
> *I am doing something brand new, something unheard of. Even now It sprouts and grows and matures. Don't you perceive it? I will make a way in the wilderness and open up flowing streams in the desert.*

Shortly after my birthday in January came the news of the sudden and tragic heart-breaking death of Kobe Bryant, which shocked the world. Not only did Kobe but his thirteen-year-old daughter Gianna alongside him. Gianna had a passion for basketball trying to learn everything she could from her dad and mentor as well, she wanted to be like her dad (legacy). Even though his death was tragic, he had and lived a triumphant journey despite everything he had been through the good, bad, and otherwise. He lived his life pursuing his passion, giving to others, encouraging, empowering through the love of his sport -- basketball. The daughter being with him at the time of the crash, I cannot imagine what was going through their minds. I can only imagine Kobe and Gianna together in Heaven still talking about basketball as I picture them together like one of the photos in the news that was priceless.

Do you recall one of the holiday family pictures they had taken together? They were as *The Wizard of Oz*? Before Kobe and his daughter's death, I thought about Dr. Lois Irene Evans and watching a glimpse of her funeral and the celebration her life and legacy. If I recall correctly, I remember during the service and her voice during a time she was giving a message, she said, "Faith is the substance of things hoped for, the evidence of things not seen. Yet if God has put it in your spirit, you walk in it. Don't be afraid of what God has for you speak it and walk in it."

That has stayed with me. I can also hear her saying to everyone,

I have fought the good fight, I have finished the race, I have kept the faith. 2 Timothy 4:7 NIV

The tragic deaths of approximately 25 of my fellow sisters and brothers, who have been killed without. There was an article dated 6/9/2020, "George Floyd Changed the World: Public Viewing in Houston honors the man behind the Social Justice Movement," (Jervis, 2020). The Mayor of Washington DC had Pennsylvania Avenue leading to the White House, the one who is sitting in the place of power like the *Wizard of Oz* the man behind the curtain, the Mayor had the road painted yellow in Big, Bold Letters **BLACK LIVES MATTER**. Did you hear what I said YELLOW lettering?

BLACK LIVES MATTER

On Thursday, July 30th at Atlanta's Ebenezer Baptist Church was the funeral of Congressman John Lewis. He served in the U.S. House of Representatives for Georgia's 5th congressional district for 33 years, who stood for Civil Rights and Voting Rights. Words that were spoken by our previous Presidents; Barack Obama, George W. Bush, Bill Clinton told of a man that stood tall and strong for what was right, a man of character. The scripture that Barack Obama spoke volumes referring to 2 Corinthians 4:8-9

We are hard pressed on every side, yet not crushed; we are perplexed, but not in despair; persecuted, but not forsaken; struck down, but not destroyed. NKJV

At the end, I could hear Congressman John Lewis say,

"I have fought the good fight, I have finished the race, I have kept the faith." 2 Timothy 4:7 NIV

then I said to myself, that is indeed what I would consider a true Triumphant Journey.

On that note, have to see the movie *Just Mercy* starring Michael B. Jordan, Jamie Foxx, Brie Larson, Rob Morgan, Tim Blake Nelson, Rafe Spall, O'Shea Jackson Jr. and Karan Kendrick, that tells about a gifted young lawyer fighting for equal justice in a flawed legal system? At the end, we WIN.

God is still on the throne; there is a catalyst for change coming from a place of strength and not weakness. Now when Dorothy wakes up from her sleep (dream), she is in her room surrounded by those she loves and realizes life is but a fleeting moment. We do not know the time or the hour. All the things she complained, murmured, and worried about was not as important as those who she was surrounded by when she woke up. That is what was important -- looking at the bigger picture.

Through Dorothy's journey, with the Lion her fear was defeated into courage, "Be strong, and of good courage." Through the Scarecrow, she had a different perspective; she was wiser knowing and saying, "I can do all things through Christ whom strengthens me." Then through the Tin Man, who desired a heart, through him, she became more sensitive to the Spirit not led by emotions and feelings that are temporary. We can't forget Toto her dog and faithful friend. He never left her side, reminding us we have a faithful Friend who never leaves or forsakes and loves us conditionally, and His name is Jesus the Alpha and Omega the Beginning and the End.

The Wizard who she was in search of to get back home, well, we know it is God (Yahweh) the King of Kings and the Lord of Lords, the Great I Am. Sometimes along the way, you will lose your way – but thank God, He restores and puts you back together again. He will give you instruction, "Go Home." In this season will you get your vision back? Where is home? Home is the place of origin, it is the place you believed all things are possible. Once God pulls you out, you cannot go back. Getting to the place called "There."

Dorothy's Life Lessons

1. There is no place like home (giving your life back to God) - may have strayed away, backslidden, etc. Coming back to God with a pure heart and a renewed mind (repented). Relationship(s), job, etc., does not treat you right. "Nobody can do you (me) like JESUS!"

2. Stay on the narrow path God has put before you - there will be twists and turns along the way, but do not get distracted stay focused. Trust in the Lord, and He will direct your path.

3. The thief comes to steal, kill, and destroy but God said, "He will give you life and life more abundantly."

4. Be watchful - everything that glitters is not gold.

5. We all need someone - We need each other "I Need You to Survive."

6. How is your home not just your external (looks, body), but how is your internal home (Spirit)?

7. Dorothy looked at things differently with a new perspective (renewing of the mind).

8. Dorothy was thankful for family (no matter how dysfunctional - like your marriage vows, "From this day forward, for better, for worse, for richer, for poorer, in sickness and in health, to love and to cherish, till death do us part according to God's holy ordinance." Not to forget, hold on, and not allowing anything to come in between the cracks.

9. Cherish life, memories, moments, and take nothing for granted.

We all have distinct, original, and extraordinary journeys, destinations, purposes and no one might not know us, we do not wear or have a label that everybody can see. We have met people, been places, and saw some things no one might ever know or imagined. We are still here not to just Survive but to THRIVE. Those who have left us or are no longer here with us in the natural for whatever cause or reason, they too lived a triumphant journey, some not realizing it.

No matter where you are in your journey called Life, no matter what you have gone through, going through and still may be going through, know you are not alone. It may not be where you anticipated at being in your life, but it does not take away from the life you lived and still living. Know that quitting is not an option. We fail at some things, but we are not failures. I am living in the *Overflow* by Pastor William Murphy III (Holla), may not look like it now, but in 1 Corinthians 2:9 NKJV

"Eye has not seen, nor ear heard, Nor have entered into the heart of man, The things which God has prepared for those who love Him."

To all that read this book, I wanted it to be as close to being perfect. I am not perfect, but God is so I give it my best, my all. That whoever reads it don't look at the flaws, but the content of what the message is portraying. I want it to be seen through God's eyes not man's, not man's heart but God's heart, not through man's spirit but God's spirit. This is my prayer.

Triumphant Journey

Shout unto God with the voice of TRIUMPH Shout unto God
Shout unto God with the voice of TRIUMPH
Shout unto God
Shout out with the voice of TRIUMPH
Jesus is the "**Lion of Judah**"

So, get your roar on - I am like the Lion see and hear my roar – be bold, be brave, and be courageous!

LET YOUR VOICE SPEAK TRIUMPHANTLY

Me, You, Dorothy and Toto, Scarecrow, Tin Man and the Lion are going to sing this song, and we are going to rock at it.

The songwriter Vashawn Mitchell, sings *TRIUMPHANT* remember you are!!!!

Triumphant I am not defeated
Triumphant
The battle's already won
There's a greater power in me
Triumphant I am not defeated
Triumphant
The battle's already won
There's a greater power in me

TRIUMPHANT JOURNEY ROAD JOURNAL

1. What does your life story tell about you?

_____

_____

_____

2. When life happens are you going to wither, survive or thrive?

_____

_____

_____

3. Where is your Getaway?

_____

_____

_____

4. Who has walked with you in your seasons of life?

_____

_____

_____

5. What are the songs that helped you through the different seasons of your life?

_____

_____

_____

6. What does your renovated self-look like?

_____

_____

_____

7. Where has your Yellow Brick Road led you?

_____

_____

_____

ABOUT THE AUTHOR

Doris Cole is an upcoming graduate of the University of Phoenix, majoring in Public Administration. She worked in Human Services for over thirty years and worked over thirteen years in Emergency Management, working with survivors in disaster recovery. Her passion and love are serving others in need of support and encouragement.

Printed in the United States
By Bookmasters